I0157690

The 108 Defilements

A Buddhist Journey Through the Shadows of the Mind

by Constantin Rosso Corvin

WINSOR
PUBLISHING

Winsor Publishing

First published in Great Britain in 2025
by Winsor Publishing

1st Edition

ISBN: 978-1-913881-18-4

www.WinsorPublishing.com

Table of Contents

INTRODUCTION

Buddhists have been counting their prayers and mantras on strings of 108 beads, called mala in Sanskrit or juzu in Japanese, for more than two millennia in temples, monasteries, and mountain trails. These beads are symbolic and more than just ritual implements. Every bead symbolises a defilement, or bonnō (煩悩), which is a heart-mind ailment that impairs consciousness, exacerbates suffering, and keeps sentient beings bound to the never-ending wheel of birth, death, and rebirth.

A traditional Buddhist schema for comprehending the entire range of existential, behavioural, emotional, and mental barriers that obstruct awakening is formed by the 108 defilements. They are energetic distortions rather than just vices in the moralistic sense; they are manifestations of the three poisons that underpin all suffering: ignorance (avidyā/無明), attachment (rāga/貪), and aversion (dvesa/瞋). Every defilement starts when the mind loses sight of its actual nature, which is clear, compassionate, and interconnected. Instead, it clings to illusion, reacts fearfully, or inflates the ego-self.

1

These 108 patterns may appear archaic and abstract, but they are surprisingly familiar and relevant. They include the overt (rage, greed, violence) and covert (self-righteousness, sarcasm, despair, spiritual materialism). They are the mental and emotional patterns we all come across on a daily basis, frequently without recognising them. Studying them is like starting to see them. Additionally, seeing them deprives them of their power.

Over centuries, the list itself changed. It was initially mentioned in Indian Buddhist texts, specifically in the Sarvāstivāda and Mahāyāna traditions. As Buddhism spread to China, Korea, Japan, and other places, it was further developed and improved. As part of New Year's Eve bell-ringing ceremonies (除夜の鐘, Joya no Kane), the Jōdo and Zen schools in Japan adopted the 108-count ritual, in which temple bells are struck 108 times to cleanse the previous year's impurities and start over. According to some commentarial texts, the number 108 is not random; rather, it is mathematically symbolic and is created by combining the six senses, three time periods, and two types of attachment.

However, this book is more than just a list. It serves as a mirror, a meditation manual, and an appeal for introspection. Every defilement is examined as a karmic imprint, with its causes, symptoms, and remedies gradually revealed, rather than merely as a word. To honour the teachings' cross-cultural applicability as well as their linguistic nuance, which is frequently lost in translation, each is written in three languages: English, Greek, and Japanese (with kanji and furigana). Greek provides philosophical clarity and Japanese provides spiritual precision where English is unable to convey the subtleties.

It is not about condemnation or judgement to comprehend

2

the 108 defilements. It's about being clear with compassion. In order to start walking with more freedom, we must recognise the barriers that keep us small. Naming is the first step towards liberation, as the Buddha taught. We start to remember that we are the sky that contains the storm, not the storm itself, when we recognise the forces that flow through us—not as disgraceful characteristics, but as ancient winds that pass through consciousness.

This book is intended for anyone who aspires to see clearly and love wisely, including seekers, practitioners, and meditators. It is a journey from darkness to light—not by running from the dark, but by looking fearlessly into it until it changes.

On the Origin and Symbolism of 108

At first glance, the number 108 may seem arbitrary. Why not 100, or 99, or 120?

The number 108 is not arbitrary, nor is it merely a ritual curiosity. It is a sacred and symbolic number, deeply embedded in the cosmology, psychology, and meditative disciplines of Buddhism, as well as in Hinduism, Jainism, and Eastern numerology more broadly. In the case of the 108 defilements (煩悩, bonnō), it becomes a comprehensive catalogue of the mental afflictions that cloud human consciousness and perpetuate the cycle of suffering.

But before exploring its spiritual application, we must understand that 108 functions as both a symbolic and systematic number — a way of representing totality. It implies a wholeness, a complete spectrum, a full mandala of human error and potential. In this way, it is not a condemnation, but a compassionate cartography of the human condition.

The Numerical Breakdown

Several Buddhist texts and commentaries attempt to mathematically explain how the number 108 is reached, particularly in the Sarvāstivāda and Mahāyāna traditions. The most common breakdown is this:

$$6 \times 3 \times 2 \times 3 = 108$$

In detail:

Six senses (六根, rok-kon):
In Buddhism, the six "sense bases" include not just the five physical senses (sight, sound, smell, taste, touch), but also the mind as the sixth — the origin of thoughts, concepts, and imagination.

Three reactions (三種受, san-shu-jū):
For each sense experience, the mind may respond in one of three ways:
- Attachment (好, liking)
- Aversion (悪, disliking)
- Ignorance (平, neutral or indifferent)

Two states (浄・染, jō / sen):
Each reaction can arise in one of two contexts:
- Pure (浄, jō) – from clarity and wisdom
- Impure (染, sen) – from delusion or defilement

Three times (三世, san-ze):
Finally, each defilement may be experienced in three times:
- The past (過去)
- The present (現在)
- The future (未来)

When multiplied together — 6 senses × 3 reactions × 2 states × 3 times — we arrive at 108. Thus, the number encompasses the entire field of sensory and mental experience, across time and states of purity or corruption. It is an elegant and deeply philosophical construction.

In Ritual

The most well-known ritual use of 108 in Buddhism is the Joya no Kane (除夜の鐘) — a Japanese New Year's Eve tradition where temple bells are struck 108 times, once for each defilement. As the last hour of the year unfolds, monks and laypeople gather to symbolically purify themselves of the accumulated karmic dust — each bell releasing another veil.

The number also appears in:

Mala beads (数珠 / juzu): traditional Buddhist prayer beads often have 108 beads, allowing the practitioner to recite a mantra or vow for each defilement.

Prostrations and repentance rituals, where one bows or chants 108 times to purify the mindstream.

Meditative cycles, with each defilement used as a daily focus across 108 days of reflection and transformation.

In this way, 108 is not just a number, but a practice — a way of engaging fully with the self, the Dharma, and the path toward awakening.

Symbolism Across Cultures and Traditions

Even outside of Buddhism, 108 is revered across spiritual lineages:

In Hinduism, there are said to be 108 Upanishads, 108 names of deities, and 108 sacred places.

In yogic traditions, the number reflects the connection between the individual and the universe, with 108 sun salutations often performed as a ritual offering.

In Jainism, 108 is the number of sacred figures and qualities one vows to honour or embody.

In astrology, it is said that the average distance between the Earth and Sun is approximately 108 times the sun's diameter — an echo of cosmic balance.

In mathematics, 108 is rich in geometry: it is the internal angle of a regular pentagon, a shape revered for its harmony and mystical symbolism.

In all these systems, 108 points toward wholeness, completion, and the integration of inner and outer reality.

The 108 defilements are not meant to be memorised like a catalogue of sins. They are a lens, showing us how the mind generates suffering from countless angles. By naming 108, the tradition symbolically says: every possible form of delusion is included here.

The precise number is less important than the principle: that liberation requires not ignoring defilements, but facing them, one by one, until the heart is free.

108 therefore functions as both a practical list and a cosmic reminder: that the human journey of awakening is vast, complete, and inclusive of every state of being.

A Brief History of the 108 Defilements

From Early Buddhist Psychology to a Sacred Catalogue of Liberation

The idea of mental defilements — kleshas in Sanskrit, bonnō (煩悩) in Japanese, āsava or anusaya in Pali — appears at the very heart of the Buddha's teachings. From the first turning of the Dharma Wheel, the Buddha identified mental afflictions as the primary cause of suffering, and their removal as the key to liberation.

However, the earliest suttas and discourses did not contain the precise list of 108 defilements. Instead, it developed gradually as a result of centuries of cultural adaptation, scholarly refinement, and psychological insight.

Early Foundations: The Three Poisons and Their Extensions

At the foundation of all Buddhist psychology lie the Three Poisons:
- Greed (rāga / lobha / 貪)
- Hatred (dvesa / dosa / 瞋)
- Delusion (moha / avijjā / 癡)

All suffering stems from these three, and each defilement identified in subsequent lists is interpreted as a branch, variation, or extension of these three. These roots were

8

eventually expanded into Ten Fetters, Five Hindrances, and other more complex groupings. Buddhist psychology evolved into a thorough mental map as well as an ethical path.

The Rise of Systematic Lists: Sarvāstivāda and Abhidharma Schools

Systematic taxonomies of mind and consciousness were introduced with the development of the Abhidharma traditions (both Sarvāstivāda and Theravāda). The mind was examined in these schools with forensic accuracy:

Mental states were classified as neutral, wholesome, or unwholesome.

Defilements were further divided into underlying formations, active outbursts, and latent tendencies.

Here, the number 108 most likely started to take shape—not as a list of distinct "sins", but rather as a catalogue of conditioned tendencies, each connected to particular mental objects, sense doors, and karmic outcomes. This list was diagnostic rather than moralistic. It sought to identify every potential cause of mental suffering so that each could be addressed, comprehended, and changed.

Mahāyāna and the Expansion of Psychological Depth

As Mahāyāna Buddhism gained popularity, particularly in China and India, its emphasis shifted to bodhisattva ethics, compassion, and turning suffering into wisdom. According to this theory, spiritual clarity could be attained by alchemising even the most excruciating defilements.

Texts like the Yogācārabhūmi-śāstra (Treatise on the Stages of Yogic Practice) examined layers of subconscious suffering, such as perceptual veils that prevent bodhisattva vision and seeds of defilement (vāsanā).

The 108 defilements now became symbolic and ritualised, showing up not only in psychology, but in:

- Mala beads, representing purification through repetition.
- Bell-ringing ceremonies, especially in Japan.
- Art and iconography, where they are sometimes depicted as demons or fetters.

East Asian Canonisation and the Popular 108 List

The number 108 was fixed and ritualised in East Asia, especially in China and Japan. Commentaries and encyclopaedic works have listed the specific defilements, including: The Mahayana Mahaparinirvana Sutra, The Treatise on the Perfection of Wisdom, and commentaries by Tiantai and Shingon scholars.

In the New Year's Eve ceremony (Joya no Kane) in Japan, the 108 were further ritualised by striking temple bells 108 times, one for each affliction to be released. This was not just symbolic; the list served as a means of yearly introspection and rejuvenation, encouraging both laypeople and monks to acknowledge and confess their own transgressions.

The list was offered in slightly different forms by various schools over time; some had terms that overlapped, while others had expressions that were culturally appropriate. However, the fundamental idea persisted:

To know the 108 ways the mind can suffer is to become free from them, one breath, one bell, one bead at a time.

Understanding the Structure of the List

The Six Roots and the Architecture of the Defilements

The 108 defilements (煩悩, bonnō) are not random. In traditional Buddhist thought, they are systematically organised according to the structure of human perception and consciousness. This organisation is not merely intellectual — it reflects the way our minds engage with the world, how defilements arise, and where they lodge themselves within our sensory and cognitive experience.

To truly appreciate the depth of this teaching, one must understand the six sensory "roots" (根, kon), each of which serves as a doorway through which defilements enter.

1. The Six Roots of Affliction

Buddhism teaches that we experience the world through six faculties — known as the six sense bases or roots (六根, rok-kon):

1. Eye-root (眼根, gankon) – visual perception
2. Ear-root (耳根, jikon) – auditory perception
3. Nose-root (鼻根, bikon) – olfactory perception
4. Tongue-root (舌根, zekkon) — gustatory perception
5. Body-root (身根, shinkon) – tactile sensation
6. Mind-root (意根, ikon) – thought, memory, imagination, and mental formations

Because each of these roots interacts with reality differently, they all give rise to unique defilements. While the ear may react to harshness and become resentful, the eye may be attracted to beauty and become desirous. The most profound and subtle illnesses, like nihilism, spiritual pride, or self-delusion, arise from the mind because it is the most complex organ.

Within each of the six roots, defilements are further diversified by combinations of:

- <u>Three emotional tones:</u> pleasant, unpleasant, and neutral.
- <u>Three time orientations:</u> past, present, and future.
- <u>Two forms of attachment:</u> pure and impure.
- And additional variations based on conscious and unconscious tendencies.

When these are multiplied together ($6 \times 3 \times 2 \times 3$), we arrive at the symbolic total of 108. This model serves as a comprehensive map of all the ways we can fall into suffering through any sensory or mental engagement. It reminds us that the path to liberation must address every level of our being.

Traditional Arrangement vs Practical Use

According to their root sense, the 108 defilements are grouped in some texts; for example, the first 18 are associated with the eye, the next 18 with the ear, and so on.

Other versions separate them according to moral category, psychological depth, or karmic weight.

The grouped structure is frequently maintained in monastic recitations or scholarly study in East Asian Buddhist traditions, where the list serves as a ritual formula as well as a diagnostic chart.

However, in contemporary practice, such an arrangement can obfuscate clarity and ease of access, particularly for readers who speak English.

The Structure of This Book

While this book honours the traditional six-root structure and explains it thoroughly here, the full list of defilements will be presented in alphabetical order in the main body of the text.

This choice has been made for practical reasons:

It allows for easy reference and study, particularly when returning to specific entries. It accommodates the fluid nature of English, which lacks the embedded nuance found in the original languages. And it supports readers who may use the book as a daily reflection or meditative companion, rather than a scholastic manual.

How to Use this Book

This is not a book to be read once and put away. It is a daily teacher, a meditation mirror, and an invitation to get to know yourself better than you have in the past. The

108 defilements are living energies that manifest in speech, action, emotion, and thought; they are not merely theoretical ideas. It is liberating in and of itself to name them and see them clearly, without denial or condemnation.

This book can be used in a number of ways, including as a ritual tool, contemplative journal, or spiritual resource:

1. As a Regular Routine

Think about reading one defilement every day and letting each description serve as a meditation. Consider how this specific pattern appears in your own life, maybe writing down your ideas or making a conscious effort to notice it all day long. Deeply ingrained tendencies can be loosened with just five minutes of silent contemplation.

This can also be combined with mala practice: recite the name of a defilement or its remedy as you go through each bead of a 108-bead mala (e.g., "anger... patience... anger... patience..."). In this sense, even the breath can be transformed.

2. As an Annual Cycle

Many practitioners adhere to important seasonal thresholds (such as the spring or autumn equinoxes) or the traditional 108-day cycle that precedes the New Year. This approach encourages you to experiment with one vice every day, ending the cycle with a bell ringing, a ceremonial letting-go, or a promise to act compassionately and resolutely on your newfound understanding.

The Joya no Kane tradition of Japanese Buddhism, in which temple bells are rung 108 times at the end of the year to cleanse accumulated defilements—a collective release and renewal—is mirrored in this structure.

3. Serving as a Mirror for Shadow Work

This book can be used for psychospiritual research, particularly when it comes to therapy, self-healing, or shadow work. Self-hatred, spite, vanity, and spiritual materialism are just a few of the defilements that lurk just beneath our conscious self-image. Take note of the entries that make you uncomfortable, defensive, or resistant as you read. These are frequently the exact locations where freedom and wisdom await.

This is an act of radical compassion rather than guilt. The goal is to free your humanity from unconscious patterns, not to eradicate it.

4. As a Tool for Ritual or Devotion

Every defilement can be used in a ritual of repentance or purification, such as burning incense, saying the name out loud, and letting go of the related karma through prayer or breath. You can also turn your personal work into a Bodhisattva activity by dedicating each reflection to the healing of all beings.

Consider using this book before meditation or following times of confusion, grief, or rage. Select a defilement that corresponds with your present circumstances, and allow the lessons to ground you in perspective, kindness, and clarity.

5. When Teaching or Practicing in Groups

This book can be an effective tool for group exploration

if you are a teacher, spiritual advisor, or sangha leader. Encourage dialogue, research, or group journaling about particular defilements. As a means of respecting various traditions and enhancing intercultural understanding of Buddhist wisdom, you might also investigate the trilingual format.

Many vices can be used to spark sincere, open discussion about universal human themes like jealousy, dishonesty, or despair.

A Word on Language and Translation

Three languages are used to present each defilement in this book:

- <u>English,</u> for ease of use and readability
- <u>Greek,</u> which conveys subtleties in philosophy
- <u>Japanese</u> (using furigana and kanji), respecting the richness and meaning of the East Asian Buddhist tradition

When translated into English, many of the 108 Buddhist defilements (煩悩, bonnō) seem to overlap or repeat. This is a reflection of the limitations of translation, not a mistake. Whether written in Pali, Sanskrit, or Classical Chinese, each term in the original Buddhist texts has a distinct meaning, emotional tone, and philosophical significance that frequently does not translate well into a single English word. For instance, a word that might be translated as "anger" in two different contexts might mean different things. In one context, it might mean a sudden outburst of anger, while in another, it might mean a quiet, simmering resentment. These two concepts are linguistically different in their original languages, but they combine into a single English word. Furthermore, even among seemingly similar emotions, Buddhist psychology is sensitive to the subtle differences in mental states, identifying distinct causes, intensities, and karmic implications. Because English is less accurate in this area, it can make different vices seem the same. Recognising this subtlety serves as a reminder that these lessons are about developing direct insight into the mental texture rather than merely focussing on the words.

This book isn't a list of your problems. It shows the starting point of suffering and the point at which freedom can be achieved. Fixing and conquering all 108 is not your task. All you have to do is observe, identify, and meet each one with compassion and honesty. Their spell is broken by that alone.

About the Author

Constantin Rosso Corvin was raised in a spiritually rooted household, where meditation, martial arts, and philosophy were central from early childhood.

His first encounter with Buddhist and Shinto practices came during a formative journey to Kyoto in 2016, while visiting Temples and Shrines.

After years of personal study rooted in his background in martial arts and meditative discipline, during a tumultuous period in his life, a solo trip to Japan in 2019 marked a turning point: clarity on how all these theories can be applied into practice for a better life, a better way of being, thus, he began to follow Buddhism and Shinto not only as sources of insight, but as a way of life.

Before fully dedicating himself to the spiritual path, Constantin was a professional classical musician — a pianist and professor of music theory — until 2021, when he took the leap to turn towards deeper study and dedication to this path.

His academic and creative background is as diverse as it is reflective of a seeker's spirit: from paleography and classical monody to astrobiology, herbalism, and the art of Jeet Kune Do. He is also the author of several other works under two different pen names. Yet as a seeker of Truth and Light he decided to carve his spiritual and philosophical journey under his real name.

The "108 Defilements: A Buddhist Journey Through the Shadows of the Mind" marks his first offering under his real name — an open gesture of alignment between inner and outer life.

煩
悩

乱用
らんよう

Abuse

Greek: Κακοποίηση

In the context of the 108 vices (煩悩, bonnō), abuse is the wrong use of power, words, or actions that hurts oneself or others. It includes both physical and emotional harm, but in Buddhism, the deeper meaning goes beyond what people do on the outside. It also includes the attitudes that lead to harm.

Abuse occurs when an individual acts from a position of ego-driven control, anger, or desire, neglecting the inherent interconnectedness of all beings. Abuse disrupts the equilibrium of compassion and mindfulness, perpetuating samsara through the continuation of suffering.

For example:

- Using harsh speech to humiliate someone.
- Exploiting others for personal gain.
- Misusing authority or influence to manipulate situations.

From a Buddhist perspective, abuse is rooted in the three poisons:

- Ignorance (無知 muchi) — failing to see the oneness of all life.
- Hatred (瞋 shin) — acting out of anger or resentment.
- Attachment (貪 ton) — clinging to personal power or control.

The first step to changing abuse is to recognise it in ourselves, even in small ways, like self-abuse through bad habits. This can be done through awareness, compassion, and right speech.

攻撃
こうげき

Aggression

Greek: Επιθετικότητα

In the context of the 108 vices, aggression means wanting to hurt, control, or overpower someone, either physically, verbally, or emotionally. It is not confined to overt violence; even nuanced hostility, resentment, or passive-aggressive conduct originates from the same source.

In Buddhism, anger (瞋 shin) is one of the three main poisons that keep samsara going. It causes aggression. When the mind clings to the idea that it is a separate, permanent self, it reacts defensively by attacking things that it thinks are threats to its identity or desires.

There are different kinds of aggression, such as:

- Physical aggression: harming others or destroying property.
- Verbal aggression: insults, shouting, or passive-aggressive comments.
- Internal aggression: holding grudges, wishing harm upon others, or harbouring deep resentment.

Buddhism teaches people to notice the first signs of anger before they show it to others. Mindfulness (念, ねん, nen) and compassion (慈悲, じひ, jihi) show us that aggression hurts both the person who is aggressive and the person who is aggressive, which keeps the cycle of suffering going.

To change aggression, we need to learn to be patient (忍辱, にんにく, nin-niku) and calm (捨, しゃ, sha). This lets us act from a place of clarity instead of reacting.

野心

<small>やしん</small>

Ambition

Greek: Φιλοδοξία

In the context of the 108 vices, ambition means wanting success, recognition, or power too much, not in a healthy way. It is the desire to do well for oneself at the cost of peace, kindness, or being present.

Buddhism differentiates between wholesome aspiration—the desire to foster wisdom, compassion, and liberation—and tainted ambition (染, ぜん, zen), which emerges from the three poisons:

- Greed (貪 ton) — the endless hunger for status or wealth.
- Ignorance (無知 muchi) — mistaking fleeting accomplishments for lasting fulfilment.
- Delusion (妄想 mōsō) — believing success will secure happiness or self-worth.

Tainted ambition manifests as:

- Striving for status or fame to feel superior.

- Sacrificing relationships and well-being for personal gain.
- Measuring self-worth solely through external validation.

Buddhism says that ambition keeps us stuck in samsara because the more we get, the more we want. True freedom comes from knowing that all worldly success is temporary (無常, むじょう, mujō) and can't bring lasting happiness.

You don't have to give up your goals to change your ambition. Instead, you should align them with Dharma by acting out of compassion and right intention (正思惟, しょうしい, shō-shiyui) instead of ego.

怒り

いかり

Anger

Greek: Θυμός

Anger is one of the 108 vices (煩悩, bonnō). It is the emotional turmoil that happens when we can't get what we want or when we feel like our sense of self is in danger. Anger can also show itself in ways that aren't obvious, like holding grudges, being irritated, or being resentful.

In Buddhism, anger is one of the three poisons (三毒, さんどく, sandoku), alongside greed and ignorance. It clouds the mind, distorts perception, and binds us to samsara by fuelling cycles of harm, retaliation, and suffering.

Subtle forms of anger include:

- Irritation at minor inconveniences.
- Silent bitterness when expectations aren't met.
- Judging others harshly, even internally.

The first step to change is to realise that anger doesn't last. Mindfulness (念, ねん, nen) lets us see anger rising without giving it more fuel. When you practise loving-kindness (慈, じ, ji) and compassion (慈悲, じひ, jihi), you can turn your anger into understanding.

傲慢
ごうまん

Arrogance

Greek: Αλαζονεία

In Buddhist thought, arrogance is the belief that you are better than other people in terms of worth, knowledge, or ability. Arrogance, unlike healthy self-confidence, makes us forget that we are all connected and that nothing lasts forever. This makes the idea of a separate ego stronger.

Arrogance manifests as:

- Looking down on others or dismissing their experiences.
- Believing one's opinions, status, or spiritual practice are inherently better.
- Resisting teachings or advice due to egoic pride.

Arrogance is based on ignorance, which means forgetting that all living things are impermanent (無常, むじょう, mujō) and will eventually die. It keeps us apart and stops us from being kind (慈悲, じひ, jihi).

Overcoming arrogance involves cultivating humility (謙虚, けんきょ, kenkyo), and see ourselves as part of the huge web of existence. In doing so, the boundaries between "self" and "other" begin to dissolve.

29

無神論

むしんろん

Atheism

Greek: Αθεϊσμός

The Buddhist definition of atheism as a defilement includes a rejection of the sacred, the invisible, and the transcendent in addition to a lack of belief in a god. It is the belief that spiritual wisdom, cause-and-effect, and liberation are illusions and that only the material world is real.

This shows up as:

- Denial of the results of spiritual practice, reincarnation, or karma.
- Cynicism about ethics, compassion, or awakening.
- Considering consciousness to be merely a biological or accidental phenomenon.

The Dharma requires faith (崇仰, しんこう, shinkō) in interdependence, awakening, and the depth of existence beyond form, but it does not require belief in gods.

This vice makes us oblivious to the enigma and interconnectedness of everything. It is cured by firsthand experience — of quiet, kindness, and inward change — rather than by doctrine.

The spell of doubt can be broken by even a brief silence.

卑劣
ひれつ

Baseness

Greek: Χαμηλότητα

Baseness is when someone acts in a way that is morally corrupt, dishonest, or small-minded. It means doing things for your own benefit, even if it means hurting someone else's dignity or health. Baseness is different from ignorance because it means lowering your integrity on purpose to get something for yourself.

Some examples are:

- Taking advantage of other people's weaknesses.
- Doing bad things even though you know better.
- Pursuing petty schemes fuelled by greed, jealousy, or spite.

In Buddhism, baseness comes from the poisons of greed and hatred. It happens when you stop being compassionate and your heart gets small. When we see our own baseness, it encourages us to do the right thing (正業, しょうごう, shōgō) by choosing actions that are in line with Dharma instead of our own ego.

Through self-awareness (観照, かんしょう, kanshō), we start to see that dignity doesn't come from being better than others or manipulating them; it comes from acting in accordance with the truth.

軽蔑
けいべつ

Belittlement

Greek: Υποτίμηση / Περιφρόνηση

Belittlement is the practice of routinely downplaying other people's efforts, opinions, value, or suffering. It could show up in subtle body language, speech, or thought. Fundamentally, it is the ego's attempt to elevate itself by putting others below it.

It looks like:

- Sarcastic rejection of someone's emotions.
- Believing that someone is less valuable.
- Making fun of things that other people consider sacred.

This vice frequently poses as humour, intelligence, or even "spiritual discernment." Disconnection, however, is at its core—a refusal to acknowledge the sacred in another person.

Seeing Buddha-nature in everything, even the broken, the small, and the lost, is a prerequisite for the Bodhisattva path. Since every being is a teacher, mirror, and fellow traveler, we cultivate respect (敬意, けいい, keii) for everyone, not just the noble, in order to heal this vice.

冒涜

ぼうとく

Blasphemy

Greek: Βλασφημία

In the context of the 108 vices (煩悩, bonnō), blasphemy means not only talking badly about the sacred, but also turning away from truth and wisdom in favour of beliefs that are based on the ego. It is the intentional disrespect or distortion of what goes beyond the self, whether that is the Dharma, the Buddha, or the interconnectedness of all life.

When the ego is afraid to give up, it becomes blasphemous. We may make fun of or ignore teachings that challenge us if we hold on to our own beliefs, status, or wants. In Buddhism, blasphemy can happen inside us too when we ignore our inner wisdom or deny who we really are.

This vice shows ignorance (無知, むち, muchi), which means not understanding that all beings are sacred. Reverence (恭敬, きょうけい, kyōkei) is what brings about change. It is not blind devotion, but a humble willingness to accept the truths that lead to a better life.

33

Second Version of Blasphemy

In Buddhism, blasphemy refers to disdain for the sacred, such as making fun of or defiling the Dharma, sacred texts, the path, or the enlightened ones, rather than insulting a deity. It could also involve the denial of the potential for awakening or the misuse of spiritual teachings for selfish ends.

It may show up as:

- Insulting or making fun of teachers or the Dharma.
- Posing as spiritually powerful for one's own benefit.
- Bending knowledge to support harm or superiority.

A heart devoid of humility and respect is reflected in blasphemy. It is regarded as one of the most serious karmic acts in Buddhist cosmology since it jeopardises both one's own and others' freedom.

It is healed through sincere repentance (懺悔, さんげ, sange), not out of fear, but out of love — for truth, for the path, and for all beings seeking light.

Even if we have mocked the sacred, we can return — because the sacred never turns us away.

打算

ださん

Calculation

Greek: Υπολογιστικότητα

In the context of Buddhism, "calculation" here doesn't mean math; it means plotting and scheming based on ego and self-interest. It is the mental tendency to change situations and relationships in order to get the most out of them, control the outcome, or protect the false sense of self.

Calculation is subtle. It can appear as:

- Offering kindness only to receive favours later.
- Withholding truth to control others' perceptions.
- Constantly strategising interactions to stay ahead.

In Buddhism, calculation is linked to attachment (貪, とん, tonne), which means holding on to a false sense of safety or benefit. But no matter how well we plan, impermanence (無常, むじょう, mujō) always wins. Understanding this liberates us; rather than attempting to control life, we learn to adapt to it, cultivating right intention (正思惟, しょうしい, shōshiyui) and genuine action.

35

無情
むじょう

Callousness

Greek: Αναλγησία

Callousness is the hardening of the heart — an emotional detachment from the suffering or needs of others. It arises when compassion is blocked, often as a defence mechanism against our own vulnerability. While indifference may feel protective, in Buddhism, it deepens separation and delusion.

Forms of callousness include:

- Ignoring another's pain because it feels inconvenient.
- Closing off emotionally to avoid personal discomfort.
- Treating others as objects rather than interconnected beings.

Callousness stems from ignorance — forgetting that all beings are bound by the same impermanence and longing for happiness. To dissolve it, Buddhist practice cultivates compassion (慈悲, じひ, jihi) and loving-kindness (慈, じ, ji). By softening the heart and embracing vulnerability, we reconnect with the truth of interbeing, where no one's suffering is separate from our own.

36

気まぐれ

きまぐれ

Capriciousness

Greek: Ασταθής διάθεση

Capriciousness refers to an unstable, fickle mind that shifts constantly based on mood or impulse. Spontaneity can be good, but being capricious shows a deeper restlessness—a lack of grounding and mindfulness that makes thoughts, words, and actions inconsistent.

This comes from wanting new things and not wanting to be uncomfortable. A fickle person is always looking for new things to do and doesn't care about keeping promises or going deeper in favour of short-term happiness.

In Buddhism, this instability keeps the mind from entering samadhi (三昧, さんまい, sanmai), which is the meditative stillness where insight comes. Cultivating equanimity (捨, しゃ, sha) stabilises the mind, enabling spontaneity to arise from awareness rather than impulse.

37

批判癖
ひはんへき

Censoriousness

Greek: Επικριτικότητα

Censoriousness is the compulsive urge to judge, criticise, or find fault in others. In Buddhism, discernment is important, but censoriousness is based on ego, which means wanting to make oneself look better by putting others down.

This vice manifests as:

- Constantly pointing out flaws in people or systems.
- Comparing oneself favourably to others.
- Focusing on imperfection rather than wholeness.

Being critical of others makes people feel separate and proud, which strengthens the false idea of "self" versus "other." Buddhism teaches that to get rid of it, you should cultivate compassionate understanding (慈悲, じ ひ, jihi) and remember that all beings are imperfect and always changing. We learn to speak in ways that lift us up instead of hurt us through right speech (正語, しょうご, shōgo).

自己満足
じこまんぞく

Complacency

Greek: Εφησυχασμός

The delusion that we have reached our destination and don't need to look farther, go deeper, or do more work is known as complacency. By conflating comfort with completion, it stops the journey.

It could appear as:

- Stagnation in one's work.
- Contentment with superficial comprehension.
- Thinking that enlightenment has already been attained.

Particularly for people who have advanced, complacency is alluring. However, "Strive diligently" was the Buddha's final utterance. We follow the Dharma until the day we die and beyond because it is a living path.

More love, more understanding, and more freedom to realise are always present.

驕り

おごり

Conceitedness

Greek: Αυταρέσκεια

Conceitedness is an inflated sense of one's abilities or importance. Conceitedness may appear akin to arrogance; however, it is more nuanced, stemming from an internal narrative of superiority that skews perception.

It appears as:

- Overestimating one's knowledge or virtue.
- Resisting teachings due to a belief of "already knowing."
- Seeking constant affirmation of one's worth.

Buddhism says that being conceited stops you from being open to learning, which is the way to wisdom (般若, はんにゃ, hannya). Being humble doesn't mean denying yourself; it means seeing things clearly and realising that all accomplishments and identities are temporary (無常, むじょう, mujō). We align ourselves with beginner's mind (初心, しょしん, shoshin) when we let go of our pride. This is where true insight grows.

軽蔑
けいべつ

Contempt

Greek: Περιφρόνηση

Contempt is the act of looking down upon others, dismissing their worth, experiences, or dignity. It arises when the ego creates rigid hierarchies of value, categorising people as "less than" in order to affirm its own superiority.

Subtle forms include:

- Silent judgment of someone's choices or abilities.
- Mocking differences in appearance, beliefs, or status.
- Withdrawing empathy because someone "isn't worth it."

Contempt exacerbates division and obscures the concept of interbeing — the truth that all entities are equally vulnerable to birth, suffering, and mortality. This illusion goes away when you learn to respect (恭敬, きょうけい, kyōkei) and see the Buddha-nature (仏性, ぶっしょう, busshō) in everyone.

残酷
ざんこく

Cruelty

Greek: Σκληρότητα

Cruelty is the conscious infliction of harm, whether physical, emotional, or spiritual. It is more deliberate than aggression; cruelty involves deriving satisfaction or power from causing suffering.

Examples include:

- Exploiting someone's weakness for personal gain.
- Using words to break another's spirit.
- Taking pleasure in others' pain.

Buddhism sees cruelty as a deep sign of the poison of hate. The antidote is compassionate empathy, which means understanding that hurting someone else hurts you too. Through practices like mettā (慈, じ, ji), we open our hearts and remember that everyone wants to be free from pain.

呪い

のろい

Cursing

Greek: Κατάρες

Cursing is the act of wishing someone else harm with words, thoughts, or deeds. Although curses might appear to be symbolic, Buddhism holds that reality is shaped by intention. One becomes entangled in negative karma when they direct their malice towards another.

This vice consists of:

- Verbally abusing other people.
- Silently wishing for bad luck.
- Harming through spiritual or energetic means.

The power of right speech (正語, しょうご, shōgo) and right intention (正〝ミ, しょうしいい, shōshiyui) is emphasised in Buddhist teachings. We can turn curses into blessings and release the hold of anger and resentment by substituting loving-kindness (慈悲, じひ, jihi) for harmful wishes.

冷笑主義

れいしょうしゅぎ

Cynicism

Greek: Κυνισμός

The idea that virtue is performative, goodness is phoney, and hope is naïve is known as cynicism. It is a wound masquerading as wisdom rather than clear-seeing. Cynicism, which is frequently the result of betrayal or disillusionment, numbs the heart to protect it.

It appears as:

- Mocking compassion or idealism.
- Assuming that everyone has ulterior intentions.
- Rejecting the idea that oneself or the world could change.

Cynicism is a veil that covers joy and faith in the Dharma. It may appear realistic and incisive, but it obscures the straightforward wonder of sincerity. Restoring a sense of childlike wonder (童心, どうしん, dōshin) is the cure; it is not naïve, but rather new, vibrant, and unarmed.

Hope is not illusion. It is the heart remembering what is still possible.

堕落

Debasement

Greek: Υποβάθμιση / Ηθική παρακμή

The act of degrading oneself or others by immoral decisions, ideals, or deeds is known as debasement. It appears when integrity is willingly compromised for short-term gains or pleasures.

Among the examples are:

- Pursuing goals without considering the repercussions.
- Sacrificing morals in order to gain money or gain favour.
- Engaging in behaviours that harm one's body, mind, or soul.

According to Buddhism, debasement results from an attachment to pleasure and a disregard for one's intrinsic worth. Transformation starts with choosing actions that are in line with virtue (徳, とく, toku) and remembering the value of human life (人身難得, にんしんなんとく, ninshin nantoku).

詐欺
さぎ

Deceit

Greek: Δολιότητα

Deceit is the deliberate deception of others for one's own gain. It reinforces distrust and distance by giving others a false reality to influence their choices or perceptions.

Forms consist of:

- Lying to conceal intentions.
- Putting on a false front in order to acquire authority or respect.
- Abusing the trust of others.

Buddhism teaches that in order to be free, one must be truthful (正語, しょうご, shōgo). Because deceit obfuscates both inner clarity and external reality, it ties us to karmic cycles. Harmony between oneself and others is restored when one practices compassion and honesty.

欺瞞
ぎまん

Deception

Greek: Παραπλάνηση

Although the terms deceit and deception are frequently used interchangeably, deception in this context refers more generally to warping reality, including not only lying but also influencing events to influence opinions. It is a more profound pattern of truth avoidance.

Deception consists of:

- Half-truths intended to manipulate results.
- Keeping information secret in order to hold onto power.
- Even self-deception, which is the refusal to recognise one's own shortcomings or motivations.

Clear seeing (見, けん, ken) and mindfulness (念, ねん, nen) are the opposites. We liberate ourselves from the tiresome task of upholding illusions when we accept reality as it is.

妄想
もうそう

Delusion

Greek: Αυταπάτη

Delusion, as used in Buddhism, is the term for holding onto skewed perceptions that result from ignorance and confusing illusion with reality. It is a profound misinterpretation of the essence of life, not just a simple misunderstanding.

Forms of delusion include:

- Thinking that material belongings or social standing are the source of happiness.
- Assuming that what is transient is permanent.
- Disregarding the fact that all living things are interconnected.

It is believed that delusion is the primary poison that gives rise to anger and greed. Developing wisdom (般若, はんにゃ, hannya) — perceiving reality as it is, devoid of projections — is the first step towards liberation.

Second Version of Delusion

自己欺瞞

じこぎまん

Self-delusion

The last veil is self-delusion, or the inability to see ourselves clearly. Even though they imprison us, the web of falsehoods, roles, defences, and identities we create to shield the ego is what it is.

It looks like:

- Assuming we're more advanced than we actually are.
- Denying the shadow parts of our minds.
- Putting our story ahead of reality.

Self-delusion cannot be broken by will alone — only by honest reflection, courageous humility, and the mirror of sangha (community). As the Buddha said, "You must know yourself to free yourself."

嘲笑

ちょうしょう

Derision

Greek: Χλευασμός

Derision is the act of making fun of or disparaging other people. Derision, as opposed to simple humour, aims to lower one's dignity, frequently in order to elevate oneself.

Among the examples are:

- Publicly humiliating someone for their errors.
- Secretly enjoying the misfortune of others.
- Employing wit not as a bridge but as a weapon.

Pride and insecurity are the root causes of derision, which prevents us from showing compassion. Derision becomes understanding when one practices kindness (愛語, あいご, aigo) and acknowledges the intrinsic value of all beings.

名誉欲
めいよよく

Desire for Fame

Greek: Επιθυμία φήμης

The craving for fame reflects a deep attachment to recognition and external validation. It traps us in cycles of comparison, constantly seeking approval to affirm our worth.

According to Buddhism, this kind of desire results in suffering since reputation is ephemeral and contingent on circumstances outside of our control. The desire for belonging in the heart cannot be satiated by fame, even when it is achieved.

Cultivating contentment (知足, ちそく, chisoku), finding joy in simplicity, and living in accordance with the Dharma rather than the world's changing opinions are the paths to freedom.

絶望

ぜつぼう

Despair

Greek: Απόγνωση

The deepest collapse of the heart is despair, which is the conviction that there is no hope for recovery, that pain never ends, and that the light has vanished. It is the death of hope, not sadness.

Desperation is regarded in the Dharma as a perilous turning point because it shuts the doors to all endeavour, practice, and compassion.

It appears as:

- Indifference to suffering.
- Abandoning a path or a vow.
- Withdrawal from life itself in silence.

Even despair, though, is temporary. Suffering is the seed of its own demise, according to the Buddha's teachings. The thread of life can be restored by meditation, community (僧, そう, sō), and even the smallest act of kindness.

飲酒癖
いんしゅへき

Dipsomania

Greek: Διψομανία

In the Buddhist context, dipsomania refers to a deeper attachment to intoxication — the desire to escape reality through substances, sensations, or altered states — rather than just excessive alcohol consumption. It shows a wish to numb pain or steer clear of spiritual and emotional discomfort.

This vice results from craving (貪欲, とんよく, tonyoku), where the mind turns to ignorance instead of wisdom for solace. While temporarily enjoyable, intoxication impairs discipline and dulls awareness, making it challenging to practice proper mindfulness (正念, しょうねん, shōnen).

To overcome this defilement, one must learn to live in clarity and presence and confront suffering without repressing it. In order to truly be free, one must transform their suffering with compassion and wisdom (般若, はんにゃ, hannya).

不和

ふわ

Discord

Greek: Διχόνοια

Discord is the disruption of harmony — whether in families, communities, or within oneself. It is a manifestation of division, fuelled by pride, miscommunication, or stubborn clinging to views.

Buddhism holds that harmony (和, わ, wa) is necessary for both daily life and the spiritual community (sangha). Discord draws us apart and away from connection. It appears when we place more importance on being correct than being kind, or when we project our internal conflicts onto other people.

To overcome discord, one needs to practice patience (忍辱, にんにく, ninniku), right speech (正語, しょうご, shōgo), and the readiness to view other people as fellow travellers rather than as obstacles.

不敬

ふけい

Disrespect

Greek: Ασέβεια

Disrespect arises when we fail to honour the dignity of others or the sacredness of life itself. It includes words and actions that diminish value, as well as internal attitudes that disregard the interconnectedness of all beings.

This vice frequently results from ignorance or egoistic pride, which forgets that everyone is a reflection of the Buddha-nature, regardless of background or level of education. Disrespect can take many forms, such as rolling our eyes, interrupting, rejecting lessons, or making fun of wisdom customs.

In Buddhism, reverence (ね敬, きょうけい, kyōkei) refers to a humble acknowledgement of the sacred rather than mindless obedience. We can dissolve the false boundaries of superiority and return to the heart of compassion by bowing, either literally or figuratively, to others, to the Dharma, and to the present moment.

不満

ふまん

Dissatisfaction

Greek: Δυσαρέσκεια

The silent pain that lies beneath a lot of human existence is dissatisfaction, the conviction that what is available is never sufficient. The incapacity to completely rest in what is is the core of dukkha (苦, く, ku), or suffering, according to Buddhist teachings.

It appears as:

- Yearning for what other people possess.
- Restlessness in silence.
- Persistently seeking fulfilment via spiritual, relational, or material means.

Although craving is the root cause of dissatisfaction, delusion — the belief that something "out there" can ultimately fulfil us — also contributes to it. Buddhist practice gently reminds us to look inward, embrace contentment (知足, ちそく, chisoku), and realise that happiness comes from how we relate to each moment rather than from what we have.

独断

どくだん

Dogmatism

Greek: Δογματισμός

Dogmatism is the inflexible adherence to one's opinions, beliefs, or interpretations despite suffering or the truth. It results from the ego's need to feel confident, in control, or superior. According to Buddhism, it is an expression of attachment to viewpoints (見取著, けんしゅちゃく, kenshuchaku).

Dogmatism manifests as:

- Ignoring the opinions of others without being receptive.
- Mistaking ideas for firsthand knowledge.
- Forming an attachment to the Dharma itself.

Ironically, if adhered to too strictly, even Buddhist teachings can turn into dogma. The Buddha cautioned against confusing the finger pointing to the moon with the actual moon. When we are prepared to let go of our opinions in order to see things from a different perspective, true wisdom emerges.

Second Version of Dogmatism

教条主義
きょうじょうしゅぎ

Dogmatism

Rigidly adhering to a belief, doctrine, or ideology in the face of experience, compassion, or wisdom is known as dogmatism. It is clinging to form as the truth eludes it, forgetting the moon and grabbing at the finger.

It manifests as:

- Insisting there is only one path or truth.
- Quoting scriptures without living their essence.
- Using teachings to judge, control, or limit others.

The Buddha said: "Do not accept my teachings blindly. Test them for yourself." The Dharma is a raft, not a prison. Dogmatism arises from fear and the need for certainty. But true wisdom requires emptiness — the willingness to see anew.

To dissolve dogmatism is to return to beginner's mind (初心, しょしん, shoshin), where every sutra is a fresh breath, and every being a revelation.

支配
しはい

Dominance

Greek: Επιβολή

The desire to exert control over others, to assert authority, and to shape the world to suit our preferences is referred to as dominance. According to Buddhist analysis, it originates from fear and an attachment to control, even though it frequently assumes the appearance of strength or leadership.

It shows up as:

- Imposing choices on other people.
- To quell dissent, speak louder.
- Manipulating circumstances or people in order to feel safe.

Buddhism holds that true strength comes from not clinging, from trusting life's course instead of trying to control it. The path of right action (正業, しょうごう, shōgō) teaches us to act with integrity rather than imposition and to view leadership as compassion in action rather than control.

権力欲

けんりょくよく

Eagerness for Power

Greek: Δίψα για εξουσία

An overwhelming desire to rule, ascend, and exert influence — not to serve, but to have authority over other people or systems — is what is meant by eagerness for power. It stems from the delusion that having power brings stability, security, or self-worth.

This desire is referred to as upādāna (取, とり, tori) in Buddhism, which means grasping. Even spiritual power turns into defilement if it is sought for self-improvement. Fear of impermanence is the root cause of the ego's desire for power as it seeks to establish itself through authority.

All power, though, is conditioned and transient. The Dharma teaches that true mastery is found in controlling oneself rather than controlling others. We let go of the need to control and start leading with wisdom and compassion by being humble (謙虚, けんきょ, kenkyo) and having the right intention (正 ゛ミ, しょうしい, shōshiyui).

厚顔
こうがん

Effrontery

Greek: Θράσος

Effrontery is a brazen, unabashed disrespect for respect, humility, or boundaries. It appears when self-awareness gives way to egoic entitlement and confidence is turned into arrogance.

It could appear as follows:

- Assuming authority and speaking over others.
- Acting impolitely and without regard for the repercussions.
- Disregarding the dignity or comfort of others in order to express oneself.

Pride and delusion—taking boldness for genuineness—are the main causes of this vice. However, in the Dharma, humility balances strength, and compassion balances clarity. Introspection (内観, ないかん, naikan) softens effort, bearing in mind that genuine dignity requires no performance.

利己主義

りこしゅぎ

Egoism

Greek: Εγωισμός

The idea that one's needs, opinions, or experiences are fundamentally more significant than those of others is known as egoism. It maintains the appearance of separation and is one of the fundamental manifestations of delusion.

Egoism can appear as:

- Claiming credit without assigning blame.
- Rejecting shared responsibility or empathy.
- Making oneself the centre of every circumstance.

According to Buddhism, the "self" is a flow of causes and conditions rather than something that is fixed or independent. Because it upholds a myth, egoism causes suffering. We can break free from the ego's hold and discover true freedom in connection by engaging in practices like selflessness (無我, むが, muga) and compassionate action (慈悲行, じひぎょう, jihigyō).

嫉妬
しっと

Envy

Greek: Φθόνος

When we are troubled by the success, happiness, or material belongings of others, envy develops. It is the mental anguish of comparison, which has its roots in the misconception that happiness is elusive and that our own value or fulfilment is somehow diminished by another's success.

Buddhism views envy as a type of resentful craving (貪瞋, とんじん, tonjin), in which aversion and desire coexist. It destroys relationships and undermines inner peace by substituting resentment for gratitude.

This vice may be imperceptible:

- Quiet displeasure over good news from a friend.
- Hoping in private that someone will trip.
- Comparing one's own worth to that of others.

Muditā (喜, き, ki) — sympathetic joy — is the cure. We move from scarcity to abundance, from separation to interconnection, when we celebrate the joy of others as if it were our own. In actuality, other people's happiness is an invitation to awaken together rather than a threat.

過剰

かじょう

Excessiveness

Greek: Ὑπερβολή

Excessiveness is the inability to find balance or moderation, whether in desires, habits, emotions, or expression. It is the urge to go beyond what is wholesome, to overdo, overconsume, or overreach, often as an attempt to fill an inner emptiness.

This vice arises from greed (貪欲, とんよく, tonyoku) and restlessness (掉挙, じょうこ, jōko), the mind's tendency to grasp at more — more food, more validation, more stimulation.

Among the examples are:

- Overindulgence in enjoyment.
- Talking excessively, loudly, or without awareness.
- Repetitive behaviours that are obsessive.

Buddhism promotes the Middle Way (中道, ちゅうどう, chūdō), in which the heart is not governed by indulgence or denial. We find enoughness, spaciousness, and the grace of restraint along that middle path — not as repression, but as a way to show compassion for both ourselves and other people.

不信

ふしん

Faithlessness

Greek: Απιστία

Faithlessness in the Buddhist sense is not merely doubt, but a lack of trust in the Dharma, in others, or in the unfolding of life itself. It is the heart's closed refusal to believe that awakening is possible — for oneself or for anyone.

Wounds are often the cause of disloyalty:

- A track record of disappointment or treachery.
- A heart that has been hardened and is resistant to weakness.
- A mindset trained to anticipate futility or failure.

However, blind faith is not required by Buddhism. It encourages us to develop trust (信, しん, shin) through firsthand encounters. Here, faith is a soft assurance that arises from awareness — the knowledge that all beings have Buddha-nature (仏性, ぶっしょう, busshō), and that everyone can follow the path to emancipation.

Moving from a lack of faith to faith is about allowing the heart to soften enough to try again, not about giving up on reason.

偽り

いつわり

Falseness

Greek: Ψευδότητα

Living or speaking in an inauthentic, dishonest, or insincere manner is referred to as falseness. Pretending to be someone one is not or saying something one does not genuinely believe are examples of it. It is a break from integrity and from truthfulness (真実, しんじつ, shinjitsu) in Buddhist practice.

Falsehood can manifest as:

- Pretending to be someone else in order to win acceptance.
- Hiding the truth in order to influence how people perceive it.
- Leading a life that isn't consistent with one's inner values.

This vice results from attachment and fear — fear of vulnerability, rejection, or failure. Falseness, however, separates the self into what we are and what we show. In order to overcome it, we go back to the path of authentic presence and right speech (正語, しょうご, shōgo), which enables the self to be seen — imperfect, yes, but real. We find the courage to be whole when we are honest.

宿命論

しゅくめいろん

Fatalism

Greek: Μοιρολατρία

The idea that nothing can be changed, that pain is unavoidable, and that effort is pointless is known as fatalism. Although it may appear to be wise, it is actually hopelessness masquerading as realism.

This vice can be found in:

- Stating, "This is just who I am."
- Giving up before attempting.
- Denying agency because of fate or karma.

Buddhism teaches that everything can change because everything is subject to cause and effect (因縁, いんねん, innen). Even the most sinister past is not a jail. It is a field where awakening seeds can be sown.

Fate is not fixed. The Dharma is the path of liberation.

陰険
いんけん

Furtiveness

Greek: Υπουλότητα

The propensity to act covertly, with ulterior intentions, and frequently in ways that are dishonest or self-serving is known as furtiveness. It is deliberate withholding of the truth to obtain an advantage or evade responsibility, not just discretion.

Among the examples are:

- Forming covert plans to control or exclude other people.
- Displaying an external smile while concealing animosity or plots.
- Expressing one intention while saying another.

Mistrust of other people and of life itself is the root cause of this vice. It displays the idea that being open is a sign of weakness and that in order to survive, the truth must be concealed.

However, truth is strength in the Dharma. Honest behaviour (誠実, せいじつ, seijitsu), understanding that vulnerability fosters real connection, and having clear intentions cultivate the foundation for compassion and trust are all ways to transform furtiveness.

多言

たげん

Garrulity

Greek: Φλυαρία

The urge to talk excessively and mindlessly, usually to fill a void, divert attention, or allay fears, is known as garrulity. In Buddhism, speech is considered sacred, but unconsidered speech becomes noise that obstructs vision.

Among the components of garrulity are:

- Speaking to control others or space.
- Speaking out of nervousness or a fear of being silent.
- Sharing without consideration or nuance.

This vice results from egoic grasping and restlessness (掉挙, じょうこ, jōko). Right speech in Buddhist practice entails self-control, mindfulness, and consideration. Silence (沈黙, ちんもく, chinmoku) is not emptiness but potential; it is the space where wisdom speaks and presence grows.

Taming garrulity means speaking with purpose, compassion, and peace rather than becoming silent.

貪食
たんしょく

Gluttony

Greek: Λαιμαργία

The excessive attachment to food and consumption that stems from cravings and indulgence rather than from a need for nourishment is known as gluttony. According to Buddhism, gluttony is a sign of a deeper hunger, one that is not limited to the body but also includes the unfulfilled mind that turns to material pleasure for solace.

It looks like:

- Eating too much in spite of being full.
- Numbing emotional pain with food.
- Obsessing over quantity and taste.

This vice emerges from greed (貪欲, とんよく, tonyoku). Liberation lies in the practice of moderation (中道, ちゅうどう, chūdō) and gratitude, seeing food as a gift to sustain practice — not a tool to satisfy endless desire.

貪欲
とんよく

Greed

Greek: Απληστία

One of the three primary poisons (燦楤, さんどく, and sandoku) is greed, which also serves as the foundation for numerous other defilements. It is the obsessive need to obtain, own, or consume something even when there is no need or advantage.

Greed manifests as:

- Obsession with material possessions, wealth, or status.
- Disregarding what we already have in favour of wanting more.
- Taking carelessly from the Earth or other people.

Because this craving is insatiable — the more we grasp, the more we hunger — it causes suffering. According to Buddhism, contentment (知足, ちそく, chisoku) is a state of freedom rather than resignation, where the heart rests in the sufficiency of the present.

恨み

うらみ

Grudges

Greek: Μνησικακία

Grudges are a type of frozen anger that is preserved in memory and are the lingering effects of past hurt. Keeping a grudge turns wounds into chains, binding us to those times and the people who hurt us.

Buddhism views grudges as a kind of clinging, not to pleasure but to suffering, even though they frequently feel justified.

Forgiveness (許し, ゆるし, yurushi) is the first step towards healing; it is not forgetting but letting go. Through compassionate insight, we realise that letting go is the only thing that can set us free.

苛慷
かこく

Harshness

Greek: Σκληρότητα

The propensity to treat people or ourselves harshly, critically, and without empathy is known as harshness. It displays a mindset that prioritises justice over comprehension and control over empathy.

It may appear as follows:

- Being ruthlessly severe or aloof.
- Speaking carelessly and cruelly.
- Refusing to be soft, even when it's required.

Harshness, which is sometimes confused with strength, is actually the result of pride, fear, or unresolved pain. True strength in Buddhism is gentle and stems from karunā (悲, ひ, hi), which is compassion that acknowledges suffering and works to alleviate it.

憎しみ

にくしみ

Hatred

Greek: Μίσος

Hatred is the intense dislike or rejection of another person, thing, or circumstance. It is one of the three poisons that come from a mindset that views other people as enemies, threats to be eliminated rather than sentient beings.

Hatred burns both ways. It eats away at the heart that contains it, warping perception and making separation worse.

Its antidote is mettā (慈, じ, ji) — loving-kindness. By recognising the suffering beneath hatred, and responding with openness rather than opposition, we begin to heal not just ourselves, but the very world we once rejected.

偽善
ぎぜん

Hypocrisy

Greek: Ὑποκρισία

The vice of feigning to have virtues or values that one does not actually possess is known as hypocrisy. It occurs when words and deeds are not in harmony, typically in an effort to gain influence, prestige, or approval.

Among the examples are:

- Acting cruelly while preaching compassion.
- Displaying a sacred image while harbouring impurities.
- Blaming others for flaws we keep hidden from ourselves.

Sincere practice in Buddhism is hindered by hypocrisy. Since awakening is about seeing clearly and living honestly, despite our flaws, rather than about seeming pure, the path calls for humility and authenticity.

幻
まぼろし

Illusion

Greek: Ψευδαίσθηση

In Buddhism, illusion is not merely magical or visual; it is the very fabric of ignorance (無明, むみょう, mumyō), the conviction that what we see as self, world, permanence, and control are stable and real.

It consists of:

- Holding that the self is fixed and distinct.
- Mistaking feeling for reality.
- Seeking long-term fulfilment from outside sources.

According to the Dharma, all compounded things are both luminous and empty (空, くう, kū). To hold on to an illusion is to suffer. However, being able to see through illusion is freedom, not nihilism.

悪意
あくい

Ill-will

Greek: Κακοβουλία

The mental state of wishing someone else pain, misfortune, or harm is known as ill-will. It is a type of active aversion that strengthens karmic ties and reinforces the illusion of enemies, whether it is concealed or expressed.

It appears as:

- Covert pleasure in the failures of others.
- Curses uttered in silence out of frustration.
- Choosing brutality over compassion.

Cultivating compassion (慈悲, じひ, jihi) — not sentimentality, but the obvious realisation that all beings strive for happiness—heals this vice. When we realise this, we see only suffering hearts, just like our own, instead of enemies.

焦燥
しょうそう

Impatience

Greek: Ανηπομονησία

The internal conflict that demands "now", "faster", and "different" is impatience, which is the refusal to accept things as they are. It results from aversion to the present and attachment to results.

It appears as:

- Annoyance with delays.
- Slow or silent agitation.
- Annoyance when our timeline isn't met by progress.

Patience (忍耐, にんたい, nintai) is a potent virtue in Buddhist practice. It is radical acceptance rather than passive waiting, a readiness to be totally present in life as it unfolds without pushing it along.

無斟心
むかんしん

Indifference

Greek: Αδιαφορία

Indifference is a numbing of the heart, a turning away from other people's joy, suffering, or humanity. It frequently results from exhaustion, fear, or overwhelm rather than malice. Nevertheless, it separates us from other people.

It could appear as follows:

- "It's not my issue."
- Disregarding cruelty or injustice.
- Emotional distance from those you love.

Buddhism encourages us to awaken from apathy by practicing compassion and mindful presence. We get back to the reality that we are all connected when we give ourselves permission to feel again, even when it hurts.

無礼

むれい

Insolence

Greek: Προσβολή

Rudeness that stems from pride or disdain is called insolence. It is the wilful or reckless disrespect for the dignity of others, frequently disguising it as bravery or self-assurance.

When we disregard the fundamental respect (恭敬, きょうけい, kyōkei) that all sentient beings deserve, it can manifest itself in speech, body language, or silence.

We become insolent when we lose sight of the fact that everyone possesses Buddha-nature, regardless of their appearance, social standing, or religious beliefs. By practicing humility, we bring respect back to our relationships and speak from our common humanity rather than our superiority.

頑固
がんこ

Intransigence

Greek: Αδιαλλαξία

The strict refusal to change, adapt, or take into account different viewpoints is known as intransigence. It is an ego-bound resistance to change, motivated by pride, fear, or stubbornness, rather than being grounded in principles. This rigidity, which clings tenaciously to form and opinion, even in the face of truth or harm, causes mental suffering in the Dharma.

This vice frequently manifests as:

- Refusal to accept responsibility or change course when incorrect.
- Rejecting novel concepts or lessons that go against one's comfort zone.
- Defending one's identity, convictions, or customs out of habit rather than wisdom.

According to Buddhism, wisdom is adaptable, like bamboo, which can sway in the wind despite having firm roots. While awakening results from being receptive and open, intransigence fights impermanence. By practicing right view (正見, しょうけん, shōken), we learn to relax, soften our certainty, and let truth emerge beyond our personal preferences.

不敬虔

ふけいけん

Irreverence

Greek: Ἔλλειψη σεβασμού

A lack of respect for what is holy, significant, or venerable — not just in terms of customs or lessons, but also in the way we handle life itself — is irreverence. It is a type of spiritual negligence in which we disregard the mystery, wisdom, or dignity of people and circumstances. It is frequently cloaked as scepticism or indifference.

In Buddhist practice, reverence is mindful respect (恭敬, きょうけい, kyōkei), which acknowledges that every moment has the capacity for awakening.

Irreverence can manifest as:

- Rejecting the Dharma as "merely concepts."
- Considering spirituality as a show or a way to achieve selfish goals.
- Disregarding the sanctity of both one's own and other people's lives.

In order to overcome irreverence, we must learn to bow inward — not out of duty, but rather out of a humble understanding of transience, interconnectedness, and the potential for change in every interaction.

無責任

むせきにん

Irresponsibility

Greek: Ανευθυνότητα

Irresponsibility is the refusal to accept responsibility for our words, deeds, and the results of those deeds. It comes from a wish to avoid discomfort or to distance oneself from the karma we create, but doing so only serves to exacerbate confusion and discord.

It frequently looks like:

- Pointing the finger at others for our errors.
- Evading responsibilities by lying or making excuses.
- Breaking promises or commitments.

In Buddhist ethics, accountability is about alignment and clarity rather than guilt. Choosing to face life consciously, mindful of the consequences of our actions, is an act of right effort (正精進, しょうしょうじん, shōshōjin).

We honour the reality that every moment is a chance to sow the seeds of liberation by taking on responsibility.

We always have the option.

嫉み

ねたみ

Jealousy

Greek: Ζήλια

The painful idea that we are less deserving because someone else has something we don't — love, success, beauty, or wisdom — is called jealousy. In contrast to envy, it frequently involves a fear of being ostracised or replaced. Buddhism holds that attachment to one's self-image and the illusion of separateness are the root causes of jealousy.

It arises in thoughts like:

- "They don't deserve that — I do."
- "If they succeed, I lose."
- "Why not me?"

Because we feel that their gain threatens our own, jealousy causes suffering rather than because others have something. Muditā (喜, き, ki) is the remedy; it is the capacity to celebrate other people's success as though it were our own. By doing this, jealousy turns into freedom and love ceases to be competitive or conditional.

批判的

ひはんてき

Judgmentalness

Greek: Επικριτικότητα

The obsessive tendency to categorise people into worthy and unworthy, good and bad, is known as judgmentalness. Despite the importance of discernment, judgmentalness stems from egoic comparison, in which we project our pride or discomfort onto the environment.

It could appear as:

- Critiquing someone's behaviour, appearance, or path.
- Evaluating individuals internally according to their perceived flaws or values.
- Applying moral principles as means of division rather than wisdom.

Buddhist practice teaches us to examine ourselves first and to reflect on our own shortcomings by looking in the mirror. Compassion breaks down barriers, whereas judgement hardens the heart. As we engage in proper mindfulness (正念, しょうねん, shōnen), we start to view other people as fellow emancipationists rather than as things to be judged.

色欲
しきよく

Lust

Greek: Λαγνεία

According to Buddhism, lust is more than just an intense desire for bodily pleasure, particularly sexual desire; it is also a mental and emotional obsession with gratification as the means of achieving fulfilment. Lust turns people into things and constricts consciousness into a tunnel of hunger.

This vice consists of:

- Obsessive thoughts about bodies or pleasure.
- Utilising other people to fulfil one's desires.
- Letting passion take precedence over reason, morality, or empathy.

Greed and delusion — the false notion that pleasure will satisfy desire — are the root causes of lust. But lust burns brighter the more we feed it. Transformation through awareness is the way out, not repression. Desire returns to its original source when we acknowledge the transience of sensations and develop spiritual intimacy (親しみ, したしみ, shitashimi) with life itself. This is the yearning for union — with truth, with presence, and with peace — rather than for consumption.

悪
あくい

Malice

Greek: Κακία

Malice is the deliberate attempt, by words, deeds, or silent thoughts, to injure, wound, or cause suffering to another being. It is different from ill-will in that it is intentional; rather than being a reaction, it is a decision to act out of hatred or retaliation.

A deeply deluded mind that confuses dominance for peace or retaliation for justice is the source of malice. Even though it might feel good at the time, it poisons both the giver's and the recipient's hearts.

According to the Dharma, hatred can only be eradicated by love (慈, じ, ji). Malice must be transformed by going back to the source of suffering, both our own and that of others, and realising that there are no enemies in reality — only suffering beings. True peace starts here.

策略
さくりゃく

Manipulation

Greek: Χειριστικότητα

Under the guise of charm, reason, or seeming kindness, manipulativeness is the use of subtle control, deceit, or influence to further one's own objectives. In contrast to overt aggression, manipulation is covert and calculated, stemming from the idea that people are merely tools and that honesty is too weak of a means to achieve things.

It consists of:

- Concealing information to influence results.
- Leverage through emotional appeal.
- Seeming giving in order to win support or favour.

This vice is a reflection of a lack of faith in both life and other people. Manipulation in Buddhism exposes a profound insecurity that is concealed by calculation. We must develop courage, openness, and authenticity in order to let it go; we must learn to relate from the heart rather than the mask. By doing this, we create the opportunity for a genuine, uncontrollable connection.

自己虐待

じこぎゃくたい

Masochism

Greek: Μαζοχισμός

Self-inflicted suffering, whether through harsh self-judgment, intentional sabotage, or the conviction that pain is justified or purifying, is referred to as masochism in the Buddhist context. It frequently stems from invisible trauma, guilt, or erroneous ideas of virtue and shows a profound detachment from one's intrinsic value.

This may show up as:

- Selecting toxic environments or relationships.
- Punishing oneself for previous deeds.
- Denying happiness or relaxation because one feels unworthy.

Buddhism acknowledges the reality of suffering, but it also maintains that compassion, not only for others but also for oneself, is the first step towards awakening. Metta (慈, じ, ji) is the consistent practice of loving-kindness towards the body, the mind, and the past, which dispels masochism.

Punishment does not purify us. Love is what awakens us.

猜疑心

さいぎしん

Mistrust

Greek: Καχυποψία

The tendency to assume bad intentions from people, question their sincerity, and anticipate betrayal or harm is known as mistrust. Mistrust closes the heart and sees connection as danger rather than opportunity, even though discernment is wise.

This vice develops as a result of past trauma that taught us to guard against suspicion. However, in Buddhism, this kind of defence frequently turns into a cage that keeps us apart from closeness, community, and the grace of interbeing.

Rebuilding the bridge of confidence (信, しん, shin) in oneself, others, and the Dharma is the way to heal mistrust rather than ignoring warning signs. We rediscover the joy of opening again when we learn to trust sensibly rather than blindly through mindfulness and care.

嘲弄
ちょうろう

Mockery

Greek: Εμπαιγμός

Mockery is a speech or behaviour that makes fun of other people, usually while pretending to be funny or astute. Its foundation is disdain and disengagement, a failure to acknowledge the dignity of the person being ridiculed, despite its seemingly innocuous or amusing appearance.

Pride, insecurity, or superiority are the root causes of mockery, which elevates oneself at the expense of another. By making fun of someone else's pain or individuality, it erodes empathy and strengthens delusion.

Buddhism views all living things as deserving of compassion. Our karmic imprint includes even our jokes. We learn to speak with awareness, kindness, and reverence through right speech (正語, しょうご, shōgo) and right view (正見, しょうけん, shōken) — choosing to elevate rather than denigrate, even in jest.

怠慢
たいまん

Negligence

Greek: Αμέλεια

The habit of ignoring one's obligations and failing to take care of the things that need to be taken care of, both inside and outside of oneself, is called negligence. According to the Dharma, it symbolises spiritual sloth, a deviation from the awakening path brought on by fear, indifference, or distraction.

Negligence can manifest as:

- Disregarding one's meditation practice or precepts.
- Delaying moral judgements for practical reasons.
- Failing to take care of or protect others when we have the ability to do so.

The energy of awakening, according to the Buddha, is diligence (精進, しょうじん, shōjin) — steadfast engagement with each moment rather than frantic doing. We must keep in mind that every action, no matter how minor, is a seed in order to overcome negligence. Furthermore, the Dharma's field is always fertile.

虚無主義
きょむしゅぎ

Nihilism

Greek: Μηδενισμός

The idea that nothing has value, meaning, or purpose is known as nihilism. Declaring life empty is a response to suffering and a means of putting an end to suffering. However, this perspective is a serious misinterpretation of emptiness in Buddhism.

It appears as:

- Denial of spiritual development, ethics, or karma.
- Conviction that showing compassion is pointless.
- Feeling that there is nothing sacred about life.

The truth of śūnyatā (空, くう, kū) is that things are empty of fixed self — not empty of worth. Emptiness is form, and within that paradox, we discover meaning not as fixed, but as arising through presence, love, and intention.

Nihilism collapses when we truly meet the present. In stillness, meaning reappears — not as answer, but as awareness.

執着
しゅうちゃく

Obsession

Greek: Εμμονή

Obsession is an overwhelming mental fixation, where thoughts, desires, or fears revolve endlessly and bind the mind like chains. In Buddhism, obsession is a form of clinging (執, しゅう, shū), where we lose spaciousness, perspective, and peace.

Obsession may attach to:

- A desire, a relationship, or a person.
- An imagined result or a fear.
- A conviction, concept, or persona.

It reduces our awareness and causes us to feel threatened by uncertainty. However, in reality, everything is transient, including thoughts (無常, むじょう, mujō). The key to freedom is releasing the hold. The storm subsides when we practise mindfulness (念, ねん, nen), which brings us back to the breath, the body, and the present.

耽溺
たんでき

Overindulgence

Greek: Υπέρμετρη απόλαυση

Overindulgence is the unbridled pursuit of pleasure, frequently at the expense of virtue, clarity, or health. Buddhism views overindulgence as a sign of a mind enslaved to craving, unable to find contentment without excess, even though the senses themselves are not sinful.

It can be found in:

- Compulsive drinking, eating, or stimulation of the senses.
- Compulsive behaviours that impede spiritual growth.
- Allowing pleasure to control our relationships and priorities.

The Middle Way (中道, ちゅうどう, chūdō), which steers clear of both asceticism and hedonism, is obscured by excess. Knowing that pleasure is a wave rather than a shore means that in order to overcome this vice, joy must be met with discernment and thankfulness rather than rejected.

独占欲

どくせんよく

Possessiveness

Greek: Κτητικότητα

The urge to claim people, things, or experiences as "mine" and to be afraid of losing them is known as possessiveness. It is a strong type of attachment in Buddhism that is connected to the delusion of permanence and ownership.

This vice could appear as:

- Jealous dominance in partnerships.
- Overprotectiveness or hoarding.
- Defining oneself based on possessions or authority.

Insecurity, or the belief that our stability or value depends on grasping, is the root cause of possessiveness. Holding tight, however, does not lead to true belonging. It comes from being totally present and realising that everything is shared with us and nothing really belongs to us.

We overcome this by practicing generosity (布施, ふせ, fuse), which teaches us the wisdom of letting go and the joy of giving.

偏見
へんけん

Prejudice

Greek: Προκατάληψη

The mental propensity to make assumptions about someone based on their identity, background, status, or appearance is known as prejudice. It is the tendency to close the heart and narrow the mind before seeing clearly. According to Buddhism, prejudice is a type of ignorance that inhibits compassion (無明, むみょう, mumyō).

It appears as:

- Judging the value of people by their gender, race, class, or religion.
- Devaluing instruction due to the appearance of the instructor.
- Responding to people based on stereotypes or fear.

The truth of interbeing is undermined and separation is reinforced by prejudice (相互存在, そうごそんざい, sōgo sonzai). Deep listening and mindfulness, viewing every individual as a mystery rather than a label, are its cure. Where assumptions end, wisdom begins.

97

慢
まん

Pride

Greek: Υπερηφάνεια

The exaggerated sense of self that one is superior to, more significant than, or more enlightened than others is called pride, or māna (慢, まな) in Buddhist psychology. Given that it can persist even within spiritual practices, it is arguably the most dangerous of the defilements.

It looks like:

• Comparing oneself favourably and demeaning other people.
• Cling to knowledge or achievements as a source of identity.
• Rejecting ego-challenging teachings.

Pride separates people. It shuts the door to connection, love, and education. Humility in the Dharma is openness, or the readiness to face every situation and person without armour, rather than shame. Our purpose is to be awake, not to be better than others. And when pride yields, awakening starts.

激怒
げきど

Rage

Greek: Οργή

Rage is the outburst of anger that obliterates consciousness and reason, frequently causing damage before the heart can recover. Whether it is short-lived or long-lived, it is always a fire that devours the bearer and everyone around them.

Buddhism views anger as an uncontrollable aversion that results from deep wounds, perceived injustice, or threat. But what it hits doesn't get better. Rather, it prolongs suffering by adding karmic harm to pain.

To transform rage, we practise forbearance (忍辱, にんにく, ninniku), not as suppression, but as the strength to pause. With breath, with care, we begin to recognise that behind the storm of rage is usually a hurt child, an unmet need, a silent grief. And with compassion, even the fiercest fire can be cooled.

怨恨
えんこん

Rancour

Greek: Κακεντρέχεια

The bitter, persistent hatred that never goes away is called rancour. It is a cold, settled resentment that is frequently carried for years or lifetimes rather than the sudden heat of anger. Rancour is one of the most poisonous mental states in the Dharma because it fosters the delusion of separateness, hinders healing, and makes it impossible to forgive.

This vice frequently manifests as:

• Practicing past betrayals in the mind.
• Reliving past trauma as a justification for staying closed.
• Pursuing justice or retribution long after the injury.

Buddhism says that carrying rancour is like trying to throw a burning coal, but you end up getting burned instead. Letting go (放下, ほうげ, hōge) is the way forward, but not for the benefit of the other person, but rather for your own independence.

Forgiveness in Buddhism does not mean forgetting or excusing — it means releasing the knot, choosing peace over poison.

無謀
むぼう

Recklessness

Greek: Απερισκεψία

Being reckless means not being thoughtful, considerate, or conscious of the consequences of one's actions. It is the unbridled manifestation of impulse, frequently fuelled by pride, restlessness, or the delusion of invulnerability. According to Buddhism, ignorance (無明, むみょう, mumyō) — the lack of understanding of cause and effect — is the root cause of this vice.

It can be found in:

- Putting oneself or others at risk in order to get excitement.
- Talking carelessly.
- Disregarding advice or cautions in favour of one's own satisfaction.

The Dharma encourages us to substitute thoughtful restraint and right action (正業, しょうごう, shōgō) for recklessness. To successfully navigate the path, we must understand that freedom is about acting with compassion and clarity, not about doing whatever we want.

怨み
うらみ

Resentment

Greek: Μνησικακία

Resentment is a slow-burning resistance or disapproval that frequently lurks beneath politeness. It is the heavy energy of unspoken grievance. Buddhism views it as a type of subdued rage that harms oneself and other people while being concealed by sarcasm or silence.

It appears as:

- Feeling cheated but keeping it to yourself.
- Internally reciting the tales of injustice.
- Avoiding confrontation by quietly withdrawing.

Resentment traps us in ancient karmic tales in which the past continues to influence the present. We release it by practicing compassionate boundaries and honest communication (誠実な表現, せいじつなひょうげん, seijitsu na hyōgen).

Giving pain a clear, blame-free name allows it to breathe and, frequently, to go away.

無作法
むさほう

Rudeness

Greek: Αγένεια

Being insensitive to the feelings, traditions, or dignity of others is known as rudeness. It is more than just bad manners; it is a kind of disrespect that conveys the message that "you don't matter," whether intentionally or unintentionally. According to Buddhism, rudeness results from ego and delusion, or the inability to acknowledge our common humanity.

It could appear as:

- Ignoring or interrupting other people.
- Using harsh or contemptuous language.
- Disregarding silence, rituals, or spaces.

Buddhism values both appropriate speech and appropriate presence. In contrast to rudeness, graciousness (礼儀, れいぎ, reigi) is a practice of reverence rather than a social performance. We make room for ourselves and others to be fully seen when we approach people with care.

皮肉
ひにく

Sarcasm

Greek: Ειρωνεία

Although sarcasm is frequently regarded as amusing or harmless, Buddhism recognises it as a subtly aggressive tactic masquerading as wit. It is a distorted form of speech because it frequently conveys the intention to ridicule, correct, or denigrate.

This vice consists of:

• Putting others down with irony.
• Grinning while expressing hurt.
• Concealing the truth behind a façade of cunning.

Sarcasm causes confusion and distance. It undermines trust and prevents authenticity. We learn to communicate directly, politely, and plainly in order to change sarcasm. Compassionate delivery of truth eliminates the need for a sharp edge.

懐疑

かいぎ

Scepticism

Greek: Σκεπτικισμός

In its corrupted form, scepticism is not healthy questioning but rather the persistent scepticism that hinders development and is frequently employed as a means of evading effort, trust, or surrender.

Although this vice may seem wise, it is frequently motivated by a fear of vulnerability, control, or disappointment. It keeps us outside of experience, constantly assessing but never going inside.

It appears as:

- Incessant questioning without preparation.
- Doubting instructors or lessons out of cynicism rather than investigation.
- Not having faith in one's own awakening experience.

The Dharma respects discernment. However, it also teaches faith (信, しん, shin), which is an openness of heart towards what cannot be proven but only lived, rather than blind belief.

To move beyond scepticism is to taste the Dharma directly, not just with the mind, but with the body, breath, and silence. Truth becomes real when we stop watching, and begin walking.

自己嫌悪
じこけんお

Self-hatred

Greek: Αυτοαπέχθεια

The internalised voice of violence is self-hatred, which is the conviction that one's shortcomings, imperfections, or very nature are deserving of disdain. It is a severe misinterpretation of the self and soul that transforms inherent humility into damaging shame.

This vice manifests as:

- Persistent self-criticism.
- Refusal to accept affection or praise.
- Destroying healing, practice, or relationships.

The self is neither to be praised nor despised in Buddhist practice. It should be viewed as a dynamic, transient combination of karma, body, and mind. Clinging to a fixed, false identity and holding it to a harsh standard leads to self-hatred.

The remedy is metta (loving-kindness), (慈しみ, いつくしみ, itsukushimi) — a tenderness that includes even our darkness. The Buddha said:

"You, yourself, as much as anyone in the universe, deserve your love and affection."

106

自尊心
じそんしん

Self-importance

Greek: Αυτο-σημασία

The idea that one's presence, function, or viewpoint is more important than others' is known as self-importance, and it can result in posturing, entitlement, and occasionally subtle forms of manipulation. It's pride masquerading as a purpose.

This vice manifests when:

- We demand to be the centre of attention.
- We are resistant to correction or criticism.
- We ascribe identities to positions, titles, or spiritual accomplishments.

Regardless of appearance, strength, or speech, all beings are equal in their Buddha-nature according to the Dharma. Humble service, or acting out of a desire to help others rather than out of ego, is the antidote to self-importance (奉仕, ほうし, hōshi).

We become more genuinely useful the more we let go of the need to be significant.

107

放縦
ほうじゅう

Self-indulgence

Greek: Αυτο-ικανοποίηση

The propensity to give in to every craving, justification, or emotion is known as self-indulgence; it allows momentary comfort to take precedence over long-term morality or goals. It is a lack of self-control that is frequently passed off as self-care. In actuality, it looks like:

- Defending excess or indolence as "being kind to myself."
- Avoiding the discomfort required for development.
- Allowing one's body or mind to run amok with desire.

True self-care, according to Buddhism, is based on purpose and clarity rather than transient pleasure. Discipline (持戒, じかい, jikai) is love strengthened, not punishment. We honour the most profound aspect of ourselves when we make decisions that are genuinely helpful to our awakening.

独善

どくぜん

Self-righteousness

Greek: Αυτοδικαίωση

The arrogant conviction that one's morals or opinions are superior is known as self-righteousness. It conceals pride in ideals, transforming even the truth into a weapon. It is particularly harmful in spiritual contexts because it distastes others while disguising itself as virtue.

It could appear as follows:

- Judging people for not choosing your route.
- Thinking that one is "further along" spiritually
- Correcting people without showing empathy.

The heart is hardened by self-righteousness. Buddhism encourages us to walk in humility while keeping in mind that all beings are equal in their ability to awaken, unfinished, and unfolding. Quiet is the hallmark of true wisdom. It pays attention. It bows.

快楽主義

かいらくしゅぎ

Sensualism

Greek: Αισθησιαρχία

Sensualism is the belief that beauty, taste, touch, and excitement will fulfil the heart and elevate pleasure to the highest level. Although life involves the senses, sensualism overidentifies with them, transforming the world into a buffet of fleeting pleasures.

According to Buddhism, this vice results in:

- Agitated desire.
- Reliance on stimulation.
- Loss of interest in more complex, nuanced pleasures.

In order to transcend sensualism, we must develop insight (観, かん, kan) and inner stillness (止, し, shi), realising that what we were looking for in the senses was never really about them. We already possess the beauty we seek.

酷薄

こくはく

Severity

Greek: Δριμύτητα

Excessive harshness in behaviour, discipline, or judgement towards oneself or others is referred to as severity. It frequently results from trauma, perfectionism, or misguided zeal, where one thinks that suffering purifies or that kindness is weakness.

It could appear as:

- Self-criticism without mercy.
- Harsh retribution for the shortcomings of others.
- Putting purity or order above compassion.

Even the precepts of Buddhism require gentle handling. The very things that are necessary for awakening — safety, openness, and trust — are destroyed by severity. Yes, the middle way teaches us to be firm, but never cruel. Instead of being sharp, let our path be steady.

無恥
むち

Shamelessness

Greek: Ξεδιαντροπιά

The state of acting without moral awareness, humility, or conscience is known as shamelessness. It is not a healthy sense of self-assurance or comfort, but rather a lack of regard for moral restraint — the conviction that one's actions, regardless of how damaging they may be, do not require introspection or responsibility.

This vice could manifest as:

- Repeating destructive actions without feeling guilty.
- Boasting about unethical decisions.
- As a teacher, rejecting the wisdom of shame.

According to Buddhist philosophy, shame (慚, ざん, zan) is the inner voice that emerges when we veer off course and serves as a guardian of virtue rather than a punishment. This voice is dulled by shamelessness. By cultivating right view (正見, しょうけん, shōken) and conscience (慚愧, ざんぎ, zangi), we rediscover shame as a compass that indicates awakening rather than guilt.

自己中心主義

Solipsism

Greek: Μονοσήμαντη Αυτοαναφορά

The idea that only oneself exists and that other people are mirrors, barriers, or extensions of one's inner world is known as solipsism. Compassion becomes conditional and empathy breaks down in this distortion.

It can be expressed as:

- Considering others as tools for personal development.
- Believing that the cosmos is a reflection of one's own thoughts.
- Disregarding the suffering of other living things.

Interbeing (相依, そうい, sōi) is fundamental to Mahāyāna Buddhism; there is no self, no other, only relationship. Misunderstood non-duality leads to solipsism, in which unity turns into the ego's final cover.

We only exist with, through, and among all other beings, that is the reality. Compassion is the centre of reality, not the self.

意地悪

いじわる

Spite

Greek: Κακεντρέχεια

Spite is the deliberate desire to inflict pain, discomfort, or annoyance — not in reaction to injury, but rather as a show of dominance, superiority, or retaliation. It is a tiny, savage act that is frequently concealed by civility or passive aggression.

Manifestations of spitting include:

- Subtly undermining someone.
- Purposefully refusing assistance or kindness.
- Taking pleasure in someone else's failure.

According to Buddhism, everyone aspires to be happy and free from suffering. This universal truth is betrayed by hate, which hardens the heart and increases karmic entanglement. Compassion (慈悲, じ ひ, jihi) softens it, and we learn to ask: What pain lies beneath this urge to harm? What if I decide to choose love instead?

強情

ごうじょう

Stubbornness

Greek: Πείσμα

The mind's unwillingness to change, even when confronted with knowledge, compassion, or the truth, is known as stubbornness. It is the rigidity of ego, clinging to one's own opinions, desires, or roles at all costs, rather than the firmness of commitment.

This vice manifests as:

- Refusing to acknowledge mistakes.
- Refusing assistance or direction.
- Clinging to beliefs in order to stay safe.

Fear — the fear that change will reveal weakness — is the root cause of stubbornness. True strength, however, is fluid, according to the Dharma. By listening and being humble (謙虚, けんき ょ, kenkyo), we let go of the need to be correct and become more receptive to being authentic.

軽薄
けいはく

Superficiality

Greek: Επιπολαιότητα

The tendency to approach life superficially, pursuing outward success, diversions, or appearances without introspection, presence, or depth, is known as superficiality. It is the rejection of inner life in favour of stimulation from the outside world.

It could appear as:

- Putting beauty before truth.
- Putting enjoyment ahead of reflection.
- Glancing superficially at relationships or feelings.

Restlessness is reflected in superficiality (掉挙, じょうこ, jōko) — the fear of looking inward. Using meditation (禅定, ぜんじょう, zenjō) to penetrate surface waves and reach the profound, luminous stillness of being is how Buddhists cultivate depth through stillness.

The most important things are frequently obscured by the noise.

116

猜疑

さいぎ

Suspicion

Greek: Καχυποψία

The mental habit of suspicion is mistrust without justification, implying danger or betrayal where none may be. Suspicion, as opposed to wise discernment, stems from fear, past trauma, and the conviction that one must always be on guard in order to survive.

It can be expressed as:

- Reflexively questioning other people's motives.
- Searching for ulterior intentions, even in goodwill.
- Emotional withdrawal brought on by perceived dangers.

Trust (信, しん, shin) is a type of brave openness rather than naïveté in the Dharma. The heart is imprisoned behind walls of suspicion. In order to overcome this vice, we must practise mindfulness and vulnerability, learn to see clearly but softly, and let love back in.

無神経
むしんけい

Tactlessness

Greek: Έλλειψη Τακτ / Ανευαισθησία

Lack of awareness of other people's feelings, timing, or boundaries is known as tactlessness. It may result from ignorance, but more often than not, it is a sign of self-absorption, when one speaks their truth without considering the consequences.

It appears in:

- Making unconscious hurtful remarks.
- Revealing private information at the wrong time.
- Ignoring or interfering with the vulnerability of others.

Speech must be timely, kind, and truthful according to Buddhist ethics. By practicing empathy and being mindful of context, tactlessness is changed (共感, きょうかん, kyōkan). Being truthful is insufficient; we also need to be kind.

誘惑
ゆうわく

Temptation

Greek: Πειρασμός

The pull towards what we know is foolish, dangerous, or misaligned that comes from the alluring voice of desire is called temptation. Buddhism views temptation as dangerous even though it is not evil because it frequently poses as fulfilment while actually dragging us farther away from freedom.

It could seem like:

- The desire to revert to bad behaviours.
- An unexpected yearning for what we have given up.
- Mental justifications for breaking vows or ethics.

Temptation is overcome not through force, but through insight (般若, はんにゃ, hannya) — the clear seeing that this is not what it promises to be. Through presence, we ride the wave without being carried away. Desire passes. Clarity remains.

軽率

けいそつ

Thoughtlessness

Greek: Απερισκεψία

The inability to think through the consequences of our words, deeds, or silence is known as thoughtlessness. It's similar to sleepwalking in that we go through life without realising the impact we have.

It appears in:

- Impulsive speech or behaviour.
- Accidentally causing harm to others.
- Failing to consider what is actually needed in a situation.

Every moment is an opportunity to sow the seeds of karma, according to Buddhism. Vigilance (念, ねん, nen)— the subtle yet ever-present awareness of our existence in the world — replaces thoughtlessness.

To live thoughtfully is to live reverently.

虚栄心

きょえいしん

Vanity

Greek: Ματαιοδοξία

The attachment to one's image, the desire to seem admirable, attractive, or impressive to others, is known as vanity. It turns the self into a performance rather than a presence and conflates appearance with value.

It could appear as:

- Obsession with praise, reputation, or appearance.
- Obscuring the truth for the benefit of society.
- Evaluating oneself based on praise from others.

Buddhism holds that genuine beauty is not found in appearance, style, or social recognition, but rather in the brightness of wisdom and compassion. Simplicity, contentment, and service calm vanity and enable the ego to dissolve into something much more radiant: authenticity.

報復心

ほうふくしん

Vindictiveness

Greek: Εκδικητικότητα

The intense desire to inflict pain on those who have wronged us, not just to obtain justice, is known as vindictiveness. The self is defined by harm and retaliation, and it is vengeance motivated by rage and attachment to identity.

It appears in:

- Imagining revenge.
- Behaving cruelly in the name of "justice."
- Clinging to injuries as an excuse for aggression.

Retaliation, however, ties us more firmly to the suffering we want to avoid, according to Buddhism. Forgiveness, equanimity (捨, しゃ, sha), and a profound understanding that healing comes from freedom rather than punishment are the paths to liberation.

Let go, not to excuse — but to rise beyond.

暴力
ぼうりょく

Violence

Greek: Bία

The deliberate infliction of physical, emotional, or energetic harm is known as violence. According to Buddhism, violence is a violation of the fundamental truth of interconnectedness, even though some may defend or retaliate with it. We hurt ourselves when we hurt someone else.

It consists of:

- Physical violence or mistreatment.
- Cruelty through dominance or behaviour.
- Using force to exert control or will.

Hatred and delusion are the root causes of violence, which is fuelled by karmic conditioning, helplessness, and fear. The remedy is ahimsa (non-harming), (不殺生, ふせっしょう, fusesshō), which is developed via compassion, self-control, and the understanding that all living things strive for peace.

True strength never needs to strike.

123

浪費

ろうひ

Wastefulness

Greek: Σπατάλη

Wastefulness, which is frequently motivated by indulgence or disconnection, is the reckless or excessive use of resources, time, or energy. It appears when we view the world not as a gift to be honoured but as something to be consumed.

It appears as:

- Excessive use of resources, food, or space.
- Ignore other people's or the environment's needs.
- Considering all sacred energy, including one's own, as expendable.

Buddhism holds that everything is sacred because it is impermanent (無常, むじょう, mujō). To waste is to lose sight of this reality. We align with simplicity, reverence, and the commitment to leave no harm behind through mindful stewardship (慎重, しんちょう, shinchō).

意志薄弱

いしはくじゃく

Weak-willedness

Greek: Ασθενής Θέληση

The inability to maintain practice, direction, or intention in the face of difficulty is known as weak-willedness. The absence of spiritual resolve (精進, しょうじん, shōjin) is what causes effort to wane and inertia to take hold, not gentleness.

This vice could appear as:

- Swiftly breaking promises or precepts.
- Giving in to indolence or temptation.
- Ignoring insight and not acting on it.

Stability, rather than perfection, is the way to awakening. Small, regular acts of discipline, reflection, and enjoyment in the process can strengthen a weak will. Even the Buddha took things one step at a time.

退却

Withdrawal

Greek: Υποχώρηση / Απομάκρυνση

Retreating from life out of fear, avoidance, or despair is withdrawal in its defiled form. It is a retreat from accountability, community, or development rather than a wise silence or sacred solitude.

It looks like:

- Escaping when someone confronts them.
- Avoiding pain or strong feelings.
- Abandoning commitments, people, or paths too soon.

Buddhism encourages retreat as a means of rejuvenation but cautions against retreating as a means of escape. We learn when to sit still and when to move forward, even if it means trembling, by practicing courage and right effort (勇気, ゆうき, yūki).

世俗的

せぞくてき

Worldliness

Greek: Κοσμικότητα

Excessive devotion to material possessions, social identity, status, and sensory pleasure is what is meant by worldliness. It represents a samsara-bound mind that looks for purpose in transient, outside, and constantly changing things.

This vice manifests as:

- Obsession with success, fame, or money.
- Putting appearance before sincerity.
- Distracting oneself from impermanence and death.

The Buddha left a palace because it was unsatisfactory (苦, く, ku) when clung to, not because the world is evil. When we realise that joy comes from depth rather than glitz and that freedom comes from letting go rather than from acquiring, worldliness vanishes.

憤怒
ふんぬ

Wrath

Greek: Έντονη Οργή

Often associated with a sense of moral justification or perceived betrayal, wrath is rage that has been sharpened into self-righteous fury. Wrath is persistent and consuming, with the goal of punishing, controlling, or destroying, in contrast to transient anger.

It could appear in:

- Violent moral crusades.
- Tantrums that result in long-term damage.
- Identifying with righteous outrage.

According to the Dharma, anger is a reflection of misdirected fire, or strong energy. Its antidote is compassion and equanimity (捨, しゃ, sha), which transform rage into defence rather than destruction. Instead of using hate to defend, the Bodhisattva uses love.

切望

せつぼう

Yearning

Greek: Λαχτάρα

Often associated with a desire for fulfilment, completion, or an imagined future, yearning is the intense, agonising longing for what is not. Despite its beauty, longing keeps us confined to the absence; it never stops reaching.

It appears as:

- Imagining success, love, or peace "out there."
- Living in the past or "someday" feeling unfulfilled right now.

This type of thirst is known as tanhā (渇愛, かつあい, katsukai) in Buddhism. The path teaches us to find the true object of longing in awakening itself, rather than to give it up.

We can't find the peace we're looking for elsewhere.

狂信

きょうしん

Zealotry

Greek: Φανατισμός

Zealotry is the strong, unquestioned devotion to a leader, doctrine, or belief that frequently results in harm, intolerance, or dogma in the name of purity. It closes the mind to truth beyond its boundaries and transforms faith into fanaticism.

It can be found in:

- Condemning people for taking different routes.
- Defending injury in the name of conviction.
- Sacrificing empathy in the name of "rightness"

Buddhism warns against this by teaching non-attachment to opinions and the Middle Way (見に執着しなぴこと, けんにしゅうちゃくしないこと, Ken ni shuuchaku shinai koto). Quiet, open, and developing are characteristics of true insight.

The Dharma is a door, not a wall.

精神的物質主義
せいしんてきぶっしつしゅぎ

Spiritual Materialism

Greek: Πνευματικός Υλισμός

The last and most dishonest defilement is spiritual materialism, which is the use of spiritual practice to bolster rather than to dissolve the ego. That's when the path turns into a mask, a status symbol, or a possession.

It includes:

- Collecting teachings like trophies.
- Using insight or meditation to appear superior.
- Mistaking altered states for awakening.

Spiritual materialism is the ego's last resort. The self may cling even in renunciation — to image, to "holiness," to being perceived as awakened.

The antidote is radical honesty, humility, and emptiness. We must release even the attachment to non-attachment. As the Heart Sutra reminds us:

"No attainment, and no non-attainment."

The true path leaves no trace — only peace.

www.ingramcontent.com/pod-product-compliance
Lightning Source LLC
Chambersburg PA
CBHW032005040426
42448CB00006B/495